This Book Belongs To:
____